Looking at Citizenship & PSHE
Book 2 A Good Citizen
Godfrey Hall
Illustrated by Peter Rigg

Contents

1. Who am I?
2. Making a choice
3. What is a friend?
4. Taking action
5. Helping others
6. Getting help
7. Part of a community
8. Making rules
9. Voting
10. Resolving conflict
11. Being different
12. My rights
13. Spotting bullies
14. Why does it happen?
15. What can we do to stop it
16. Working against bullies
17. The right to vote
18. Newspapers, television and radio
19. Staying safe
20. Listening to others
21. Why have laws?
22. Saying no
23. Stop it
24. Theft

No part of this publication may be reproduced in any form other than by the original purchaser. Only direct photocopies from this master are permitted. No sale of these photocopies is permitted. No copyright rights are extended or implied to secondary users.

ISBN 1 84198 221 0 © Godfrey Hall 2003
Published by Learning Materials Ltd, Dixon Street, Wolverhampton, WV2 2BX
www.learningmaterials.co.uk
Tel: 01902 454026 Fax: 01902 457596
e-mail: learning.materials@btinternet.com

Who am I?

Fill in these details:

Name: _____

Birthday: _____

Family: _____

Pets: _____

Favourite food: _____

Favourite football team or pop group: _____

I would like to be: _____

Draw a picture of yourself doing something you enjoy.

What makes you happy? _____

_____

Making a choice

Making a choice is very important. Different people can help you with your decision. Which choices can these people help you with?
Tick the correct boxes.

	The time you get up?	The food you eat?	Dealing with a bully?
parents	☐	☐	☐
brother or sister	☐	☐	☐
best friend	☐	☐	☐
teacher	☐	☐	☐
yourself	☐	☐	☐

Would any of these help you make a choice or decision?

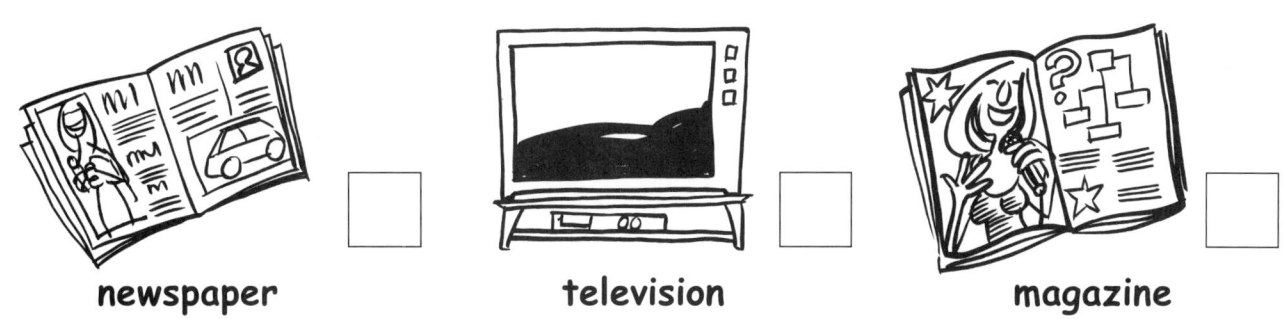

newspaper ☐   television ☐   magazine ☐

What is a friend?

Describe someone you admire.

_____
_____
_____

Colour each quality you think a friend should have.

I would want a friend to be:

- honest
- helpful
- unreliable
- trustworthy
- understanding
- quiet
- noisy
- good looking
- kind
- fun

How could a friend help you if this happened? _____
_____
_____
_____
_____
_____

Taking action

As you get older you have to make more and more decisions and choices. Look at the pictures below. Write down what decision you would make if you saw these things happen.

_____

_____

_____

Discuss your decisions with other pupils.
Tick the correct boxes.

Do they agree with you?	Yes ☐	No ☐
If you had talked to them first would you have changed your mind?	Yes ☐	No ☐
Did you make the right decision?	Yes ☐	No ☐
Do you think other people can influence your decision?	Yes ☐	No ☐

Helping others

Sometimes other people find it difficult to make a decision.
What advice could you give if this happened?

A friend says she saw another child steal some sweets from a shop.

I would _____
_____
_____
_____
_____
_____

Someone tells you that he is being bullied at school.

I would _____
_____
_____
_____
_____
_____

Your best friend says he has been offered drugs.

I would _____
_____
_____
_____
_____
_____

A classmate has been asked if she would like to smoke a cigarette.

I would _____
_____
_____
_____
_____
_____

Explain why it is important to be a good listener. _____
_____

Getting help

If you have a problem you may need help.
Colour in the people who could help out if this happened.

1. Someone steals your mobile phone.

police officer   firefighter   nurse   shopkeeper

2. You are knocked over and injure your arm. You cannot move.

paramedic   lorry driver   young child   old lady

3. Another child is bullying you at school.

teacher   doctor   parent   firefighter

4. Find out the local phone numbers of:

a doctor _____   a hospital _____

a dentist _____   the emergency services _____

Part of a community

We are all part of a community in school and outside. As part of this community we belong to clubs and groups.

List below the clubs and groups you could join.

School	Outside

Now draw an activity that you might take part in at one of these clubs or organizations.

What could you get out of being a member?

_____
_____
_____

Making rules

Do you think it is important to have rules? Explain why.

_____
_____
_____

Look at the rules below.
Tick the ones you think would be useful
if you were out on your bicycle.

- Always ride on the left. ☐
- Make sure that you signal clearly. ☐
- Always stop at a green light. ☐
- If someone is on a crossing, stop and let them cross. ☐
- Your bike should always have lights on it when it is dark. ☐

Now add two extra rules. _____
_____

Make up a set of five rules that could be used in your classroom.

1. _____
2. _____
3. _____
4. _____
5. _____

Why do you need rules at school? _____
_____

Voting

Voting is a fair and democratic way of deciding something. The government is elected by a system of voting. Candidates are elected if they have more votes than anyone else. Voting usually takes place in a local hall or school.

- Have a vote in class on your favourite food.
- Write the names of five popular foods on the chart.
- Call out each name and let people vote.

Food	Number of Votes

The favourite food was _____

SECRET BALLOT

Hold a secret ballot to find out which is the favourite pop idol of your group.

- Write the names of 4 pop stars on the ballot paper below.
- Copy the ballot paper so everyone in your group has one.
- Ask everyone in your group to put a cross next to their favourite pop star.
- Ask everyone to fold their ballot papers and put them in a box.
- When everyone has voted, open the box and count the votes.
- Announce the winner.

BALLOT PAPER	

Resolving conflict

Sometimes, when you are with friends it is difficult to decide what to do.
At home, you might argue with your family about which TV channel to watch.

Draw a line to link the start of each sentence with its end.

If my friend wants to see one film and I want to see another	toss a coin.
	scream.
If we are bowling and we have to decide who goes first we	we just discuss it with each other.
It is important if you have a difference of opinion	for help from an adult.
	make up.
When you disagree with someone you may	get upset.
	to listen to the other person's point of view.
When there is a serious argument at school you might ask	sulk.

Write a short story about a disagreement you had with a friend or relative.

Being different

Whilst it is good to be part of a gang or group it is important to remember that you are an individual. You have your own views and ideas.

Tick the things you could do to make sure that you stand out as an individual.

- wear what you want to wear ☐
- have your own opinions ☐
- not give in to others ☐
- go off on your own ☐
- listen but not always agree ☐

Complete these sentences about people who want to be different.

Wayne liked wearing _____

Chloe enjoyed listening to the music of _____
because _____

Shaun enjoyed being on his own in his room because _____

Kylie dyed her hair because _____

Draw a picture of either Wayne or Kylie.

My rights

We all have rights both at school and at home.
Look at this list of rights you might have at school.
Underline the five you think the most important.

- Teachers should listen to your questions.
- Bring your own chair into the classroom.
- Go out of the classroom at anytime.
- Stay in at lunchtime.
- Speak when you want to.
- Have a space for your coat.
- Have up-to-date books.
- Eat what you like in class.
- Wear what you like.
- Do what you like in lessons.
- Hear what the teacher says.
- Have a modern classroom.

Choose two of these rights which you think would be unworkable. Explain why.

1. _____
   _____
   _____

2. _____
   _____
   _____

Write down three rights you think you should have at home.

1. _____
2. _____
3. _____

Spotting bullies

Bullies come in all shapes, ages and sizes.
They like to pick on people and get their own way.
Colour in the people below who could be bullies.

Tick the people you think could be described as bullies.

Paul	He likes helping people.	☐
Dawn	She picks on younger children.	☐
Robert	He tries to hurt other people for fun.	☐
Sarah	She pushes people around and is always calling them names.	☐
Daniel	He says horrible things about people and talks about them behind their backs.	☐
Kirsty	She is friendly and always kind.	☐

Explain how you can spot a bully.

_____
_____
_____
_____

Some bullies work in gangs. Write a story about someone being bullied.

Why does it happen?

There are many reasons why people turn into bullies.

Bullies may:
  be unhappy.
  just enjoy hurting other people by words and actions.
  come from homes where there is a lot of fighting.
  need to feel in control.
  like other people watching them.

Match the sentence and the phrase.
Stick them on a piece of paper.

| Bullies like to be in |
| Often bullies haven't any |
| Bullies can be |
| They like |
| Children at risk are those |
| Bullies don't like children who are |

| hurting other people. |
| control of others. |
| smaller than others in the group, new or maybe having problems at home. |
| old or young. |
| cleverer than they are. |
| friends or people that like them. |

Draw a picture of **someone being bullied**.

What can we do to stop it?

It is possible for people to help stop bullying.
What could these people do to help stop it?

POLICE OFFICER

_____
_____
_____
_____

TEENAGERS

_____
_____
_____
_____

SHOPKEEPER

_____
_____
_____
_____

TEACHER

_____
_____
_____
_____

Who else might be able to stop bullying? _____

Working against bullies

It is possible to work together to stop bullying.
Look at the pictures and complete the stories.
Show how you can work with others to stop bullies.

You are walking along the road with two friends when two children who are known as bullies approach you.

_____
_____
_____

John is walking down the road. Another boy who is known as a bully, brushes past him and knocks his bag to the ground.

_____
_____
_____

Jane is walking along the corridor with Raza when two children walk by and make a racist remark.

_____
_____
_____

Sally and Jill are in the classroom when another girl comes in and picks up Sally's pencil case and walks out of the room with it.

_____
_____
_____

Work on an anti-bullying assembly to show to the rest of the school.

The right to vote

When there is an election nearly everyone in the United Kingdom has the right to vote for members of the House of Commons. The party that wins the most seats becomes the Government.

Look at the words in the box and fit them into the spaces below.

```
fair    secret    Member of Parliament    1928
     10 Downing Street      House of Commons
     Prime Minister    polling station    London
```

When you vote it has to be _____.

When you vote in a general election you do it in _____.

Women got the vote in _____.

Voting takes place at a _____.

The leader of the Government is called the _____.

MPs sit in the _____.

The letters 'MP' stand for _____.

The Prime Minister lives at _____.

The Houses of Parliament are in _____.

Name your local MP. _____

Which party does he or she represent? _____

Newspapers, television and radio

We read newspapers, watch television and listen to the radio.

On a separate piece of paper write a report of this robbery from a shop.

 a) for a local newspaper (it must not be more than 75 words).

 b) for a local television station (it must not be longer than 30 seconds)

How are these reports different?

___

___

Explain why.

___

___

Read the reports to the class and ask them what they think happened.

Staying safe

Look at the two pictures below.
Put the correct safety tips next to each drawing.

- Be careful. People on chat lines may be lying.
- Do not give out your address or phone number.
- Go out with your friends and come back with them.
- Make sure your parents know where you are going.
- Always leave a contact number and address.
- Do not arrange to meet someone from a chat line as it can be dangerous.

Listening to others

Which of these people could give us good advice on:

police officer

where to cross the road?

which medicine to take?

teacher

where to fit a smoke alarm in your home?

how to tackle bullies?

firefighter

how to stop your mobile phone from being stolen?

doctor

how to make an emergency phone call?

There may be more than one correct answer!

Why have laws?

Rules and laws are there so that we can be safe and live peacefully together. There are three main types of law:

- **Criminal**   • **Moral**   • **Civil**

Criminal These are to do with committing a crime.

Moral These are often religious laws to do with right and wrong.

Civil These can be to do with buying houses and problems over land.

Look at the pictures below. What kind of law is being broken?

Write an ending to this story.

The two boys stole the car from the car park. They drove it at high speed through the estate. As they turned the corner into the High Street an old lady stepped out to cross the road.

_____

_____

_____

Saying no

Remember a stranger is someone you don't know very well.

Draw a picture of a stranger below.

Run - Yell - Tell

Run - Yell - Tell

Why should you never go with strangers? _____

_____

Tick the people below who may be a 'danger stranger'.

Police officer	☐	Fire fighter	☐
Window cleaner	☐	A woman and young child	☐
Man or woman on their own	☐	A young man driving a van	☐
Your teacher	☐	A crossing warden	☐

Who could you turn to for help if you were on your own?

_____

How might someone trick you to get into your house?

_____

_____

Design a 'Say No' poster.

Stop it

Vandalism is when someone damages or destroys property. Damaging things such as fences or phone boxes can put people's lives at risk.

Look at this picture.

Now fill in these details.

Did it happen during the day or night? _____

Where did it happen? _____

Who were they? _____

Why did it happen? _____

How could you stop it from happening? _____

_____

_____

Write a poem or story called 'Actions can cost lives'.

Theft

Every year about £2 billion is lost through stealing.

How could you protect these things?

mobile phone

your home

purse or wallet

bike

luggage

What should you do if you know someone is stealing from others?

Who should you tell? _____

Have you ever felt like stealing something?
Discuss what it would feel like if someone took something belonging to you.

Name: _____

Looking at Citizenship & PSHE: Book 2 A Good Citizen
Pupil's Record Sheet

Use this sheet to record each pupil's level of understanding achieved in each of the topics addressed in this book. Place a tick or comment under the appropriate heading.

Topic	Achieved	Not achieved	Developing
1. Who am I?			
2. Making a choice			
3. What is a friend?			
4. Taking action			
5. Helping others			
6. Getting help			
7. Part of a community			
8. Making rules			
9. Voting			
10. Resolving conflict			
11. Being different			
12. My rights			
13. Spotting bullies			
14. Why does it happen?			
15. What can we do to stop it			
16. Working against bullies			
17. The right to vote			
18. Newspapers, television and radio			
19. Staying safe			
20. Listening to others			
21. Why have laws?			
22. Saying no			
23. Stop it			
24. Theft			

Copyright © 2003 Godfrey Hall, Looking at Citizenship & PSHE Book 2 Learning Materials Ltd, Wolverhampton, WV2 2BX

Permission is given to the purchasing school only to photocopy this page. This material is not copyright free.